EARLY INTERMEDIATE
ROMANTIC E

6 ORIGINAL PIANO SOLOS
by Randall Hartsell

ISBN 978-1-61774-104-3

Willis Music

Exclusively Distributed By
HAL•LEONARD® CORPORATION
7777 W. BLUEMOUND RD. P.O. BOX 13819 MILWAUKEE, WI 53213

© 2010 by The Willis Music Co.
International Copyright Secured   All Rights Reserved

For all works contained herein:
Unauthorized copying, arranging, adapting, recording, Internet posting, public performance,
or other distribution of the printed music in this publication is an infringement of copyright.
Infringers are liable under the law.

Visit Hal Leonard Online at
www.halleonard.com

FROM THE COMPOSER

The French term *étude* is defined as a study. Piano etudes usually focus on the technical skills of playing scales, chords, arpeggios, voicing, etc. From the Baroque toccata to the demanding and beautiful etudes of Frédéric Chopin, both pianists and audiences love the exhilaration of a dazzling and lyrical performance.

Romantic Etudes aims to fulfill this purpose for the intermediate student. Although Chopin resisted descriptive titles (see **Note** below), *Romantic Etudes* provides titles that will hopefully inspire spirited performances from students. Each etude emphasizes a specific technical skill with subtle harmonic and melodic changes that will appeal to the maturing pianist.

Our pleasure is presenting you with this motivating resource!

Randall Hartsell

Note: Many of Chopin's etudes did attract nicknames, such as the famous "Revolutionary" etude (Op. 10, No. 12), the sparkling "Black Key" etude (Op. 10, No. 5), and the delicate "Aeolian Harp" etude (Op. 25, No. 1)—the last coined by Robert Schumann.

for Sarah Mumford

CONTENTS

4   Etude Dramatique

7   Morning Star Etude

10   Disenchanted Etude

14   Heroic Etude

17   Ocean Etude

20   Storm Etude

24   *Biography*

Etude Dramatique

Randall Hartsell

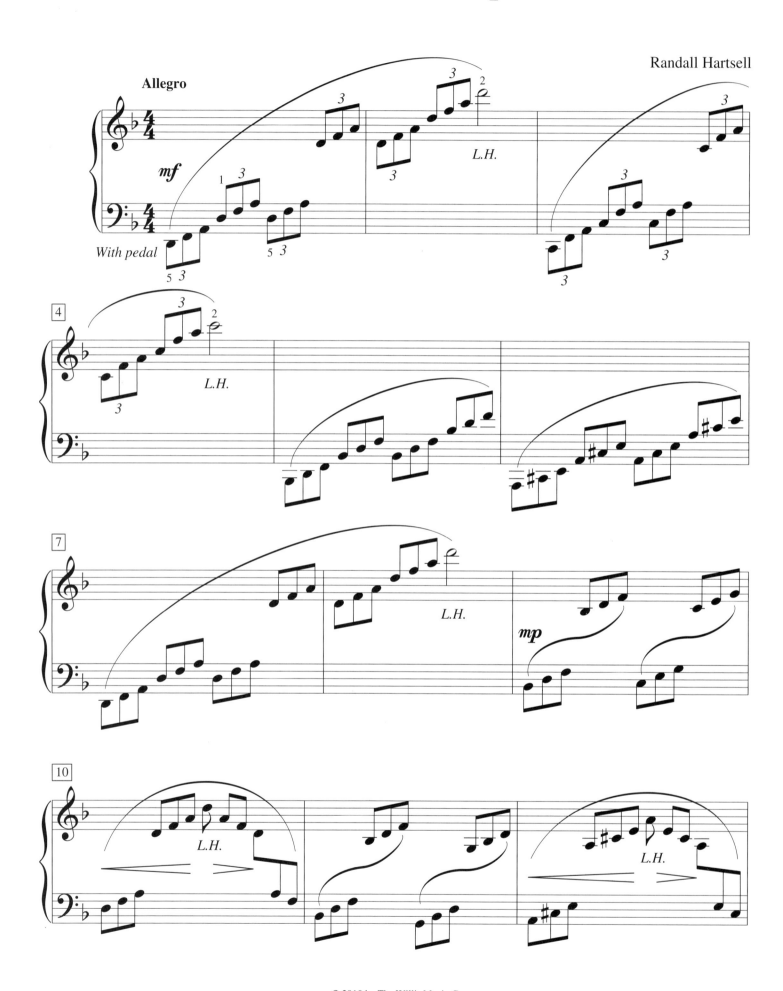

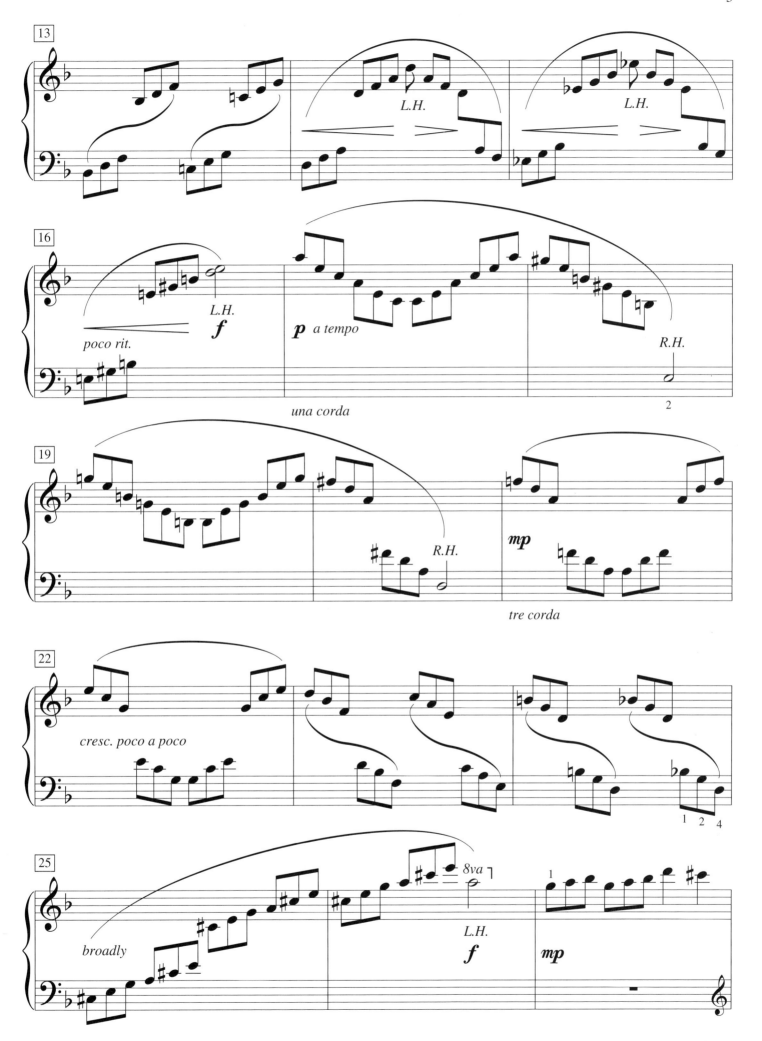

Morning Star Etude

Randall Hartsell

Disenchanted Etude

Randall Hartsell

Heroic Etude

Randall Hartsell

Ocean Etude

Randall Hartsell

© 2010 by The Willis Music Co.
International Copyright Secured   All Rights Reserved

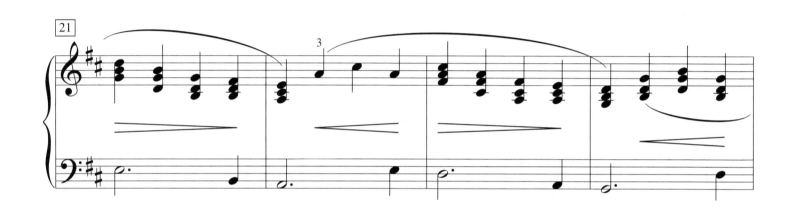
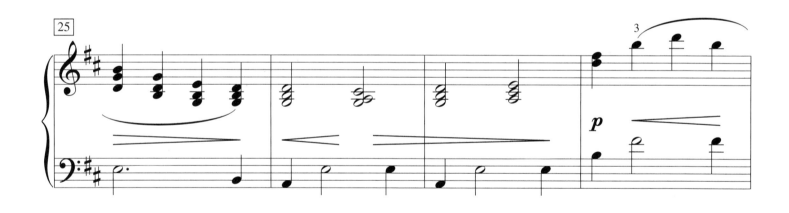
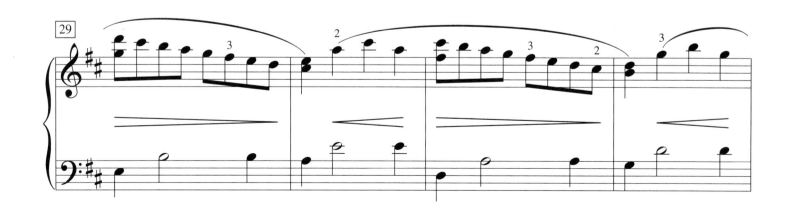

Storm Etude

Randall Hartsell

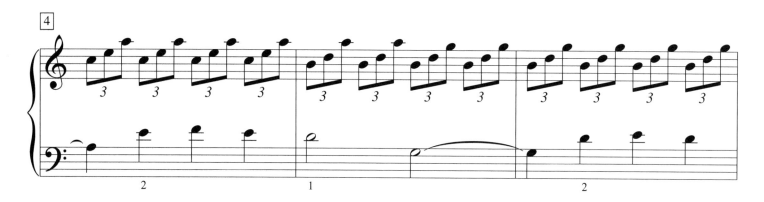
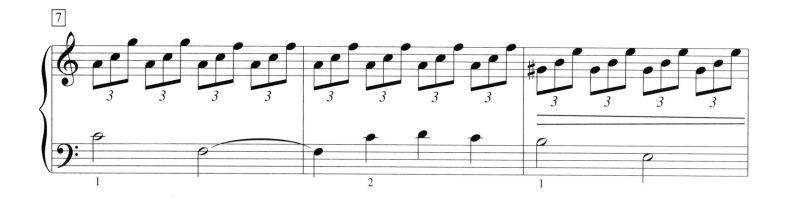

© 2010 by The Willis Music Co.
International Copyright Secured   All Rights Reserved

BIOGRAPHY

Randall Hartsell is a composer, pianist/organist, clinician and teacher from Charlotte, North Carolina. Mr. Hartsell is particularly known for his lyrical and melodic compositional style, and consistently aims to write pieces that students will love to play and teachers will love to teach! He currently operates a private studio in the Charlotte area.

Mr. Hartsell is a graduate of East Carolina University, where he majored in piano pedagogy and performance, and was previously on the faculty of the school of music at the University of North Carolina (Charlotte). He has well over 100 publications in print, and has been featured as a commissioned composer in *Clavier* magazine.

Visit *www.halleonard.com* for more works by Randall Hartsell.